_____

_____

_____

Birdie Lover Publishing

I'm very happy being me,
although sometimes I'd love to be
a bird so that I could fly.

Joy Fielding

Name of the Bird

Date:

Time

Category:

Location:

Weather:

Features & Description:

Observation Notes:

Comment:

Name of the Bird

Date:

Time

Category:

Location:

Weather:

Features & Description:

Observation Notes:

Comment:

Name of the Bird

Date:

Time

Category:

Location:

Weather:

Features & Description:

Observation Notes:

Comment:

Name of the Bird

Date:

Time

Category:

Location:

Weather:

Features & Description:

Observation Notes:

Comment:

Name of the Bird

Date:

Time

Category:

Location:

Weather:

Features & Description:

Observation Notes:

Comment:

Name of the Bird

Date:

Time

Category:

Location:

Weather:

Features & Description:

Observation Notes:

Comment:

Name of the Bird

Date:

Time

Category:

Location:

Weather:

Features & Description:

Observation Notes:

Comment:

Name of the Bird

Date:

Time

Category:

Location:

Weather:

Features & Description:

Observation Notes:

Comment:

Name of the Bird

Date:

Time

Category:

Location:

Weather:

Features & Description:

Observation Notes:

Comment:

Name of the Bird

Date:

Time

Category:

Location:

Weather:

Features & Description:

Observation Notes:

Comment:

Name of the Bird

Date:

Time

Category:

Location:

Weather:

Features & Description:

Observation Notes:

Comment:

Name of the Bird

Date:

Time

Category:

Location:

Weather:

Features & Description:

Observation Notes:

Comment:

<u>Name of the Bird</u>

Date:

Time

Category:

Location:

Weather:

Features & Description:

Observation Notes:

Comment:

Name of the Bird

Date:

Time

Category:

Location:

Weather:

Features & Description:

Observation Notes:

Comment:

Name of the Bird

Date:

Time

Category:

Location:

Weather:

Features & Description:

Observation Notes:

Comment:

Name of the Bird

Date:

Time

Category:

Location:

Weather:

Features & Description:

Observation Notes:

Comment:

Name of the Bird

Date:

Time

Category:

Location:

Weather:

Features & Description:

Observation Notes:

Comment:

Name of the Bird

Date:

Time

Category:

Location:

Weather:

Features & Description:

Observation Notes:

Comment:

Name of the Bird

Date:

Time

Category:

Location:

Weather:

Features & Description:

Observation Notes:

Comment:

Name of the Bird

Date:

Time

Category:

Location:

Weather:

Features & Description:

Observation Notes:

Comment:

Name of the Bird

Date:

Time

Category:

Location:

Weather:

Features & Description:

Observation Notes:

Comment:

Name of the Bird

Date:

Time

Category:

Location:

Weather:

Features & Description:

Observation Notes:

Comment:

Name of the Bird

Date:

Time

Category:

Location:

Weather:

Features & Description:

Observation Notes:

Comment:

Name of the Bird

Date:

Time

Category:

Location:

Weather:

Features & Description:

Observation Notes:

Comment:

<u>Name of the Bird</u>

Date:

Time

Category:

Location:

Weather:

Features & Description:

Observation Notes:

Comment:

__Name of the Bird__

Date:

Time

Category:

Location:

Weather:

Features & Description:

Observation Notes:

Comment:

Name of the Bird

Date:

Time

Category:

Location:

Weather:

Features & Description:

Observation Notes:

Comment:

Name of the Bird

Date:

Time

Category:

Location:

Weather:

Features & Description:

Observation Notes:

Comment:

Name of the Bird

Date:

Time

Category:

Location:

Weather:

Features & Description:

Observation Notes:

Comment:

Name of the Bird

Date:

Time

Category:

Location:

Weather:

Features & Description:

Observation Notes:

Comment:

Name of the Bird

Date:

Time

Category:

Location:

Weather:

Features & Description:

Observation Notes:

Comment:

<u>Name of the Bird</u>

Date:

Time

Category:

Location:

Weather:

Features & Description:

Observation Notes:

Comment:

<u>Name of the Bird</u>

Date:

Time

Category:

Location:

Weather:

Features & Description:

Observation Notes:

Comment:

Name of the Bird

Date:

Time

Category:

Location:

Weather:

Features & Description:

Observation Notes:

Comment:

Name of the Bird

Date:

Time

Category:

Location:

Weather:

Features & Description:

Observation Notes:

Comment:

Name of the Bird

Date:

Time

Category:

Location:

Weather:

Features & Description:

Observation Notes:

Comment:

Name of the Bird

Date:

Time

Category:

Location:

Weather:

Features & Description:

Observation Notes:

Comment:

Name of the Bird

Date:

Time

Category:

Location:

Weather:

Features & Description:

Observation Notes:

Comment:

Name of the Bird

Date:

Time

Category:

Location:

Weather:

Features & Description:

Observation Notes:

Comment:

<u>Name of the Bird</u>

Date:

Time

Category:

Location:

Weather:

Features & Description:

Observation Notes:

Comment:

Name of the Bird

Date:

Time

Category:

Location:

Weather:

Features & Description:

Observation Notes:

Comment:

Name of the Bird

Date:

Time

Category:

Location:

Weather:

Features & Description:

Observation Notes:

Comment:

Name of the Bird

Date:

Time

Category:

Location:

Weather:

Features & Description:

Observation Notes:

Comment:

<u>Name of the Bird</u>

Date:

Time

Category:

Location:

Weather:

Features & Description:

Observation Notes:

Comment:

Name of the Bird

Date:

Time

Category:

Location:

Weather:

Features & Description:

Observation Notes:

Comment:

Name of the Bird

Date:

Time

Category:

Location:

Weather:

Features & Description:

Observation Notes:

Comment:

Name of the Bird

Date:

Time

Category:

Location:

Weather:

Features & Description:

Observation Notes:

Comment:

Name of the Bird

Date:

Time

Category:

Location:

Weather:

Features & Description:

Observation Notes:

Comment:

<u>Name of the Bird</u>

Date:

Time

Category:

Location:

Weather:

Features & Description:

Observation Notes:

Comment:

Name of the Bird

Date:

Time

Category:

Location:

Weather:

Features & Description:

Observation Notes:

Comment:

__Name of the Bird__

Date:

Time

Category:

Location:

Weather:

Features & Description:

Observation Notes:

Comment:

Name of the Bird

Date:

Time

Category:

Location:

Weather:

Features & Description:

Observation Notes:

Comment:

<u>Name of the Bird</u>

Date:

Time

Category:

Location:

Weather:

Features & Description:

Observation Notes:

Comment:

Name of the Bird

Date:

Time

Category:

Location:

Weather:

Features & Description:

Observation Notes:

Comment:

Name of the Bird

Date:

Time

Category:

Location:

Weather:

Features & Description:

Observation Notes:

Comment:

<u>Name of the Bird</u>

Date:

Time

Category:

Location:

Weather:

Features & Description:

Observation Notes:

Comment:

Name of the Bird

Date:

Time

Category:

Location:

Weather:

Features & Description:

Observation Notes:

Comment:

Name of the Bird

Date:

Time

Category:

Location:

Weather:

Features & Description:

Observation Notes:

Comment:

__Name of the Bird__

Date:

Time

Category:

Location:

Weather:

Features & Description:

Observation Notes:

Comment:

Name of the Bird

Date:

Time

Category:

Location:

Weather:

Features & Description:

Observation Notes:

Comment:

Name of the Bird

Date:

Time

Category:

Location:

Weather:

Features & Description:

Observation Notes:

Comment:

Name of the Bird

Date:

Time

Category:

Location:

Weather:

Features & Description:

Observation Notes:

Comment:

Name of the Bird

Date:

Time

Category:

Location:

Weather:

Features & Description:

Observation Notes:

Comment:

Name of the Bird

Date:

Time

Category:

Location:

Weather:

Features & Description:

Observation Notes:

Comment:

Name of the Bird

Date:

Time

Category:

Location:

Weather:

Features & Description:

Observation Notes:

Comment:

Name of the Bird

Date:

Time

Category:

Location:

Weather:

Features & Description:

Observation Notes:

Comment:

Name of the Bird

Date:

Time

Category:

Location:

Weather:

Features & Description:

Observation Notes:

Comment:

<u>Name of the Bird</u>

Date:

Time

Category:

Location:

Weather:

Features & Description:

Observation Notes:

Comment:

Name of the Bird

Date:

Time

Category:

Location:

Weather:

Features & Description:

Observation Notes:

Comment:

Name of the Bird

Date:

Time

Category:

Location:

Weather:

Features & Description:

Observation Notes:

Comment:

Name of the Bird

Date:

Time

Category:

Location:

Weather:

Features & Description:

Observation Notes:

Comment:

Name of the Bird

Date:

Time

Category:

Location:

Weather:

Features & Description:

Observation Notes:

Comment:

Name of the Bird

Date:

Time

Category:

Location:

Weather:

Features & Description:

Observation Notes:

Comment:

Name of the Bird

Date:

Time

Category:

Location:

Weather:

Features & Description:

Observation Notes:

Comment:

Name of the Bird

Date:

Time

Category:

Location:

Weather:

Features & Description:

Observation Notes:

Comment:

Name of the Bird

Date:

Time

Category:

Location:

Weather:

Features & Description:

Observation Notes:

Comment:

__Name of the Bird__

Date:

Time

Category:

Location:

Weather:

Features & Description:

Observation Notes:

Comment:

Name of the Bird

Date:

Time

Category:

Location:

Weather:

Features & Description:

Observation Notes:

Comment:

Name of the Bird

Date:

Time

Category:

Location:

Weather:

Features & Description:

Observation Notes:

Comment:

Name of the Bird

Date:

Time

Category:

Location:

Weather:

Features & Description:

Observation Notes:

Comment:

<u>Name of the Bird</u>

Date:

Time

Category:

Location:

Weather:

Features & Description:

Observation Notes:

Comment:

Name of the Bird

Date:

Time

Category:

Location:

Weather:

Features & Description:

Observation Notes:

Comment:

Name of the Bird

Date:

Time

Category:

Location:

Weather:

Features & Description:

Observation Notes:

Comment:

Name of the Bird

Date:

Time

Category:

Location:

Weather:

Features & Description:

Observation Notes:

Comment:

<u>Name of the Bird</u>

Date:

Time

Category:

Location:

Weather:

Features & Description:

Observation Notes:

Comment:

Name of the Bird

Date:

Time

Category:

Location:

Weather:

Features & Description:

Observation Notes:

Comment:

<u>Name of the Bird</u>

Date:

Time

Category:

Location:

Weather:

Features & Description:

Observation Notes:

Comment:

Name of the Bird

Date:

Time

Category:

Location:

Weather:

Features & Description:

Observation Notes:

Comment:

Name of the Bird

Date:

Time

Category:

Location:

Weather:

Features & Description:

Observation Notes:

Comment:

Name of the Bird

Date:

Time

Category:

Location:

Weather:

Features & Description:

Observation Notes:

Comment:

__Name of the Bird__

Date:

Time

Category:

Location:

Weather:

Features & Description:

Observation Notes:

Comment:

Name of the Bird

Date:

Time

Category:

Location:

Weather:

Features & Description:

Observation Notes:

Comment:

Name of the Bird

Date:

Time

Category:

Location:

Weather:

Features & Description:

Observation Notes:

Comment:

Name of the Bird

Date:

Time

Category:

Location:

Weather:

Features & Description:

Observation Notes:

Comment:

Name of the Bird

Date:

Time

Category:

Location:

Weather:

Features & Description:

Observation Notes:

Comment:

Name of the Bird

Date:

Time

Category:

Location:

Weather:

Features & Description:

Observation Notes:

Comment:

Name of the Bird

Date:

Time

Category:

Location:

Weather:

Features & Description:

Observation Notes:

Comment:

Name of the Bird

Date:

Time

Category:

Location:

Weather:

Features & Description:

Observation Notes:

Comment:

Name of the Bird

Date:

Time

Category:

Location:

Weather:

Features & Description:

Observation Notes:

Comment:

__Name of the Bird__

Date:

Time

Category:

Location:

Weather:

Features & Description:

Observation Notes:

Comment:

Name of the Bird

Date:

Time

Category:

Location:

Weather:

Features & Description:

Observation Notes:

Comment:

__Name of the Bird__

Date:

Time

Category:

Location:

Weather:

Features & Description:

Observation Notes:

Comment:

Name of the Bird

Date:

Time

Category:

Location:

Weather:

Features & Description:

Observation Notes:

Comment:

<u>Name of the Bird</u>

Date:

Time

Category:

Location:

Weather:

Features & Description:

Observation Notes:

Comment:

Name of the Bird

Date:

Time

Category:

Location:

Weather:

Features & Description:

Observation Notes:

Comment:

Watching birds has become part of
my daily meditation affirming my
connection to the earth body.

Carol P. Christ

Birdie Lover Publishing

Made in the USA
Monee, IL
13 December 2019

18544081R00065